TECH **TITANS**

FACEBOOK

BY GAIL RADLEY

CONTENT CONSULTANT

Dr. Sherali Zeadally
Associate Professor
College of Communication and Information
University of Kentucky

Essential Library

An Imprint of Abdo Publishing | abdobooks.com

ABDOBOOKS.COM

Published by Abdo Publishing, a division of ABDO, PO Box 398166, Minneapolis, Minnesota 55439. Copyright © 2019 by Abdo Consulting Group, Inc. International copyrights reserved in all countries. No part of this book may be reproduced in any form without written permission from the publisher. Essential Library™ is a trademark and logo of Abdo Publishing.

Printed in the United States of America, North Mankato, Minnesota.
082018
012019

Cover Photo: Thomas Trutschel/Photothek/Getty Images
Interior Photos: Shutterstock Images, 4–5, 43 (top), 47, 83, 92; Katherine Welles/ Shutterstock Images, 9; Red Line Editorial, 10, 31; Rick Friedman/Corbis/Getty Images, 12–13; Paul Sakuma/AP Images, 15, 37, 41, 43 (bottom left); Juana Arias/ The Washington Post/Getty Images, 19; Felix Mizioznikov/Shutterstock Images, 20; Sundry Photography/Shutterstock Images, 24–25; Jason Kempin/Getty Images for Common Sense Media/Getty Images Entertainment/Getty Images, 28; Krista Kennell/Shutterstock Images, 33; Alexey Boldin/Shutterstock Images, 34–35; Denys Prykhodov/Shutterstock Images, 43 (bottom right); Syda Productions/Shutterstock Images, 44–45; Angie Yeoh/Shutterstock Images, 52–53; Brian Blanco/AP Images, 56; Jeff Chiu/AP Images, 60; Jonathan Saruk/Getty Images Europe/Getty Images, 62–63; Andrew Lichtenstein/Corbis/Getty Images, 67; Annabelle Marcovici/AP Images, 71; Chandan Khanna/AFP/Getty Images, 74–75; Takehito Kobayashi/Yomiuri Shimbun/ AP Images, 78; Monkey Business Images/Shutterstock Images, 81; Jon Elswick/AP Images, 84–85; Alex Edelman/picture-alliance/dpa/AP Images, 89; Pablo Martinez Monsivais/AP Images, 95; Lewis Joly/Viva Technology/Sipa/AP Images, 97

Editor: Arnold Ringstad
Series Designer: Laura Polzin

Library of Congress Control Number: 2018948254

Publisher's Cataloging-in-Publication Data

Names: Radley, Gail, author.
Title: Facebook / by Gail Radley.
Description: Minneapolis, Minnesota : Abdo Publishing, 2019 | Series: Tech titans | Includes online resources and index.
Identifiers: ISBN 9781532116872 (lib. bdg.) | ISBN 9781532159718 (ebook)
Subjects: LCSH: Facebook (Firm)--Juvenile literature. | Social media--Juvenile literature. | Technology--Juvenile literature. | Mass media--Social aspects-- Juvenile literature.
Classification: DDC 006.754--dc23

CONTENTS

CHAPTER ONE

ORGANIZING A MOVEMENT

Teresa Shook said, "It was mind-boggling," reacting to the January 21, 2017, protest the day after President Donald J. Trump's inauguration.[1] Professors Erica Chenoweth and Jeremy Pressman would later call it "likely the largest single-day demonstration in recorded US history" in an article for the *Washington Post*.[2] Many say Shook started it. And the tool she used was Facebook.

Businessman Trump had waged an unusually divisive campaign against Hillary Clinton, who had served as secretary of state and was a former US senator. Most pollsters thought Clinton would win, ending the male-only line of presidents. Before the election, Clinton supporters were riding high. Trump's campaign had angered many groups. He spoke of banning Muslims from entering the country and limiting women's

The Women's March, held on January 21, 2017, demonstrated the power of Facebook to help activists organize and push for social change.

rights. He was also viewed as insensitive to people of color. Further, 19 women accused Trump of past sexual harassment and abuse. The media ran recordings of Trump bragging about abuse and insulting women.

However, when the election results rolled in, Trump had won 306 electoral votes to Clinton's 232. The news upset many across the nation and even beyond. Among them was Hawaii resident Teresa Shook. A grandmother and retired lawyer, Shook had never been an activist—until the night after the election. Like more than two billion others worldwide, Shook had a Facebook account. On "Pantsuit Nation," a page for Clinton supporters, she wrote out her distress, calling for a women's march at the inauguration. With help from some online friends, she set up a Facebook event page. Forty people responded. Comforted, Shook went to bed.

FROM REAL TO RIDICULOUS

Events posted on Facebook run the gamut from real and serious—like the Women's March—to imaginary and ridiculous. "Dress up like a bird and run into the glass at US Bank Stadium," comedian Cullen Ryan typed onto his Facebook Events page, calling for people to flock to a Minneapolis, Minnesota, stadium. Sometimes it is hard to tell a joke from a serious event. "Okay, I ran into 40% of the building. I'm going to be here all night," complained one respondent. Another user wondered, "how do we check in 'safe' after we run into the glass?" Within a couple of days nearly 10,000 had commented and some 1,200 pledged to participate.[3]

By the next morning, she had thousands of responses from people willing to march.

Meanwhile, in New York, a female fashion designer, Bob Bland, had a similar thought. "I think we should build a coalition of ALL marginalized allies + do this," she proposed on Facebook.[4] She encouraged people in every state to plan marches, as Shook would do in Hawaii. Bland recruited three female activists to plan what became the Women's March on Washington. "This is not an anti-Trump rally," clarified Carmen Perez, one of Bland's picks. "Trump is a reflection of what the country represents right now, but it's so much larger than him. We're not marching on Trump; we're marching on Washington."[5]

BLAND'S TEAM OF ACTIVISTS

The Women's March was a blend of several marches with different names that began separately, as Shook and Bland did. As things began to take shape, each state with its own leader worked toward creating one major event in the nation's capital. Bland was intent on including all parts of American society. She chose three experienced New York activists. Her copresident was African American woman Tamika Mallory, who had assisted President Barack Obama's staff with issues related to civil rights, health care, and policing abuse. Carmen Perez, who focuses on finding alternatives to prison sentences, particularly for youth, became treasurer. Linda Sarsour, a Muslim activist who addresses legal and diversity issues, was cotreasurer.

Bland also made it clear that men were wanted. "We welcome our male allies," she said. "We want this to be as inclusive as possible while acknowledging that it's okay to have a women-centered march."[6]

THE MARCHERS MARCH ON

Shook didn't intend for her efforts to stop with the 2017 march. The march, noted a *Slate* magazine article, "pulled more newbies into the political fold than any single event in U.S. history . . . as voters, organizers, and candidates." Although there were widespread Republican victories in the 2016 election, author Christina Cauterucci points out that in the subsequent two years there was "a surge of Democratic victories . . . across the country" along with more activism.[9] Protests against guns and police brutality followed. Furthermore, Cauterucci credits the Women's March with inspiring the #MeToo movement, in which scores of women revealed sexual harassment and abuse they had endured in the workplace and elsewhere.

Diverse groups have worked together following the march. Rather than disbanding, the Women's March organization now has full-time employees to carry on the work. Among their next areas of focus is registering voters.

GOING TO WASHINGTON

"I'm overwhelmed with joy," Shook told the more than 500,000 men and women who had gathered to march in Washington, DC.[7] "A negative has been turned into a positive. All these people coming together to unite to try and make a difference. That's what we're going to be doing for the next four years."[8] Others protested in their own towns and cities, from Florida to Alaska and California to Maine, in support of the Washington event. Combined, the protesters numbered more than four million, estimate Chenoweth and Pressman. Citizens in other regions across the globe also protested.

The sign at Facebook's headquarters in Menlo Park, California, features the company's iconic thumbs-up symbol.

The success of the protest demonstrated people's worries about Trump's election, his views, and his behavior. But it also showed something else: the power of online social networks to get an idea rolling. Many social change projects get their start on Facebook. Companies have embraced it as well. But its most frequent use comes from its vast network of individual users.

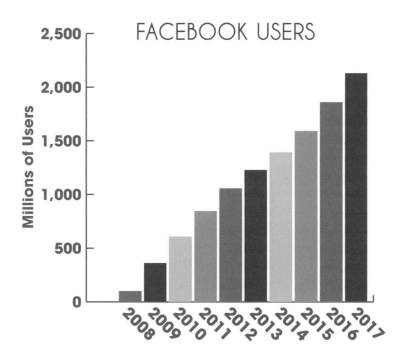

FACEBOOK USERS

Millions of Users

2,500
2,000
1,500
1,000
500
0

2008 2009 2010 2011 2012 2013 2014 2015 2016 2017

Facebook's user count has grown steadily through the late 2010s. With more than two billion users by 2018, the company now counts more than a quarter of the people on Earth as users of its service.

A GLOBAL SOCIAL NETWORK

A project that began in a college dormitory, originally meant to help college students connect with each other, averaged 1.45 billion active users each day in 2018 and employed more than 27,000 people.[10] Based in Menlo Park, California, Facebook has offices in 12 other US cities and more than 30 countries. Although a user must be at least 13 to open an account, children between ages eight and 12 told researchers in 2011 that Facebook was their second most often visited site. To include more of them, Facebook introduced an application—including parental controls—called Messenger Kids. This would help Facebook capture a fresh crop of teen and adult users in the future.

The social network's success has made Facebook founder Mark Zuckerberg one of the wealthiest people in the United States. As of June 2018, he was worth approximately $79 billion.[11] Facebook has become a household name. It is loved and hated by people of every age group and background. And at nearly every step of the way, it has been awash in controversy.

CHAPTER **TWO**

THE BIRTH OF FACEBOOK

Facebook began with a college student and his friends. Nineteen-year-old Mark Zuckerberg, a Harvard University psychology major, couldn't stop fiddling with computer projects, whether it was a program to help students pass a history final exam or one to help them connect socially. The latter, started in a cluttered college dorm, would earn Zuckerberg billions.

In 2003, with his second year barely begun, Zuckerberg invented Course Match, a program that let his classmates choose their classes based on who else was taking them. That way, they could raise their chances of getting to know someone who had caught their eye. Zuckerberg's next project was Facemash. Like most schools, Harvard took pictures of new students. It then sent collections of the photos to students'

Zuckerberg, *left*, worked with Harvard classmate Chris Hughes on the early version of Facebook.

residence halls. These directories were known as face books. Unconcerned by rules—if he knew of them— Zuckerberg hacked into the halls' files to get the pictures. One afternoon in early November, he displayed them on a new website. The home page read, "Were we let in [to Harvard] for our looks? No. Will we be judged by them? Yes."[1] The website, Facemash, invited users to rate their classmates' looks, comparing one person at a time against another. He sent the link to a few friends to test. Soon the link was leaked to others, and Facemash swept through campus.

By 10:00 p.m., Zuckerberg's computer, which hosted Facemash, was overwhelmed by users. Some people complained that the site encouraged racism and sexism. By 10:30 p.m., campus computer services shut down Zuckerberg's access. Zuckerberg had to face the Administrative Board for discipline. He had broken the college's security, copyright, and privacy rules, the board told him. They put him on probation and sent him to counseling.

The experience didn't slow Zuckerberg's inventive streak. "I had this hobby of just building these little projects," he explained later. "I had like twelve projects

MARK ZUCKERBERG

Founder Mark Zuckerberg's Facebook profile shows that he was born in 1984 in Dobbs Ferry, New York. Before Harvard, he attended a respected private high school, Phillips Exeter Academy.

With a dentist father and psychiatrist mother, Mark and his three sisters grew up comfortably. His parents encouraged Mark's early interest in technology, giving him computers and registering him for programming classes. At about age 12, Mark created what he called ZuckNet, a program to send messages between computers in the household. He also created online games, always looking for the next challenge.

Personal computers were starting to become commonplace in the 1980s, with the World Wide Web going public in 1991. Computer technology and Mark grew up together. "Sometimes it was tough to stay ahead of him," commented Mark's childhood computer tutor. "He was a prodigy."[2]

Zuckerberg makes frequent public appearances at interviews and Facebook press events.

that year," some for other students.[3] He had been writing computer programs since childhood. His passion led his parents to hire a computer tutor for him when he was about 11. Then they enrolled him in a graduate-level computer course.

A NEW PROJECT

By January of his second year at Harvard, Zuckerberg was deep into a new project. It combined aspects of Course Match, Facemash, and an existing social networking site called Friendster. He called it Thefacebook, after Harvard's photo collections.

Thefacebook was a natural outgrowth of trends at Harvard. Searching for classmates they would like to meet, students pored over the *Freshman Register,* a yearly book containing photos of first-year students. Many wished for an online version. Friendster had given them a taste of what online social networking could do—supply them with details about people and a

SYNAPSE

The final high school project of Mark Zuckerberg and roommate Adam D'Angelo was a program called Synapse. It tracked the music that the user listened to and then suggested new songs he or she might like. Synapse also caught the attention of several companies. Microsoft offered Zuckerberg and D'Angelo jobs at the company. They declined, saying they wanted to go to college.

way to connect. According to Zuckerberg, Harvard put off launching such a site because the administration was concerned about publishing student information online. But the student newspaper, the *Harvard Crimson*, kept the idea alive. One suggestion caught Zuckerberg's attention: "Much of the trouble surrounding the Facemash could have been eliminated if only the site had limited itself to students who voluntarily uploaded their own photos."[4]

By February 2004, Zuckerberg released Thefacebook to Harvard students. This time he used a commercial server to avoid more school problems. Although money had never been Zuckerberg's prime objective, he teamed up with business student Eduardo Saverin. Thefacebook began on a shoestring budget, with

THE TIME IS NOW

Social media sites had been sprouting on several college campuses but were soon eclipsed when Thefacebook came on the scene. Begun in 1999 at Amherst College, an online service called the Daily Jolt allowed students to create an unofficial website for their school with campus information and a discussion board. The template attracted students at other colleges to also establish Daily Jolts. Stanford University's Club Nexus, started in 2001, was dying out as Thefacebook arrived. Friendster, a social networking site open to the public, began in 2003. It quickly soared to several million users. However, its computer infrastructure struggled under the heavy load, and the company could not keep up. Two University of California students created Collegester, also in 2003. None of these services would have the staying power of Thefacebook.

Saverin and Zuckerberg each pitching in $1,000 for expenses. Zuckerberg had a feeling about the website's potential. In less than a week, nearly 1,000 classmates had signed on.[5] Selling advertising space to keep Thefacebook afloat was an option, but Zuckerberg was in no hurry to begin. Above all, he wanted to keep Thefacebook fun.

The original Facebook had a few simple features. Users could post one picture along with contact information, political leanings, birth date, gender, dormitory, music and reading preferences, and whether they were in or looking for a relationship. Users could add online "friends"—other users who could access their profile pages—and receive friend requests. The key feature of Course Match was preserved on the new website. Users could list the courses they were taking and search for other people by classes. They could search in other ways as well, such as by names and by class year. As users collected online friends, a visual representation of their network of connections was created, but this feature was dropped later. No other content was posted beyond what users shared about themselves.

The site also had a curious little option with no description, called poking. "We thought it would be fun

Plug-in FAQ

[thefacebook]

home search global social net invite faq logout

[My Friends]

[export]

[global]

Find friends at other schools.

Export contact informati
in Outlook and other p

[invite]

: friends to join thefacebook.

[Other Schools]   [GWU]   [All]

t Friends

Filter: [Recently Updated Profiles]

[message]   [remo

You have 247 friends.

KIP ABER
profile updated recently

[message]   [re

Steph Adams

[message]

Joshua Kumar Adlakha

The early versions of Thefacebook looked much different from the
social media services of today.

The buzz about Thefacebook quickly spread across the Harvard campus.

to make a feature that has no specific purpose," explains Zuckerberg.[6] Poke is still in use today. Users click poke on a friend's page. The friend gets a notice of being poked by their friend. It is a low-effort way of greeting someone.

Zuckerberg had learned a few things from Facemash. One was respect for people's rights and their need to have some control over their information. Students could choose the photos they posted and the details they wanted to share. Privacy controls allowed them to decide who could access the data—everyone, friends only, or those in their year at Harvard. The goal was to help people connect, not rate each other. "I know it sounds corny," Zuckerberg told a campus newspaper reporter, "but I'd love to improve people's lives, especially socially."[7]

ZUCKERBERG'S TEAM

Zuckerberg turned to his pals for help with Thefacebook. He found plenty of talent even in his dormitory suite. His first business partner, Eduardo Saverin, was the son of a rich Brazilian businessman. An officer in Harvard's investment club, he was known as a math wizard. Next came Dustin Moskovitz, a suitemate. Moskovitz was taking courses in computer science when he offered to help with the site, but he didn't yet know how to write code. He quickly learned programming. As Zuckerberg didn't like giving interviews, roommate Chris Hughes, a literature and history major, jumped in as spokesman.

FACEBOOK SPREADS

To join the site, users needed a Harvard email address. As students, alumni, and staff signed on, the number of users soared. Soon, students at other colleges wanted in. Zuckerberg hired roommate Dustin Moskovitz to

WHO HAD THE BIG IDEA?

Thefacebook was deep in controversy from the start. In fact, several of Zuckerberg's classmates sued him for what they called theft of their idea. Nearly a year before Zuckerberg created Facemash, junior Divya Narendra was dreaming of an online means of firing up his social life. He interested twin Harvard students Tyler and Cameron Winklevoss in the idea, which they called the Harvard Connection. Zuckerberg came to their attention during Facemash's drama. They hired him to help with programming. As the weeks wore on, they say, Zuckerberg gave them promises and excuses, but not work. Finally, with nothing done, Zuckerberg quit to work on Thefacebook. Zuckerberg claims his inspiration came from the school newspaper, the *Harvard Crimson*, and students' interest in online social sites. Narendra and the Winklevosses claim the inspiration was theirs. They initiated a lawsuit. In 2008, Zuckerberg agreed to give them a sizable cash settlement and stock in Facebook.

add more schools. Rather than add schools lacking an online social media service, Zuckerberg headed straight for the competition. "I wanted to go for schools that would be hardest for us to succeed at," he explained. "I knew if we had something better than the others it would make it worth putting time into."[8]

One by one, they opened Thefacebook to Columbia, Stanford, Yale, and other major universities. The site's popularity was quickly obvious. More than 2,000 Stanford students joined in the first week.[9] At first, users could connect only with people from their own schools. But because of user demand, Thefacebook changed to allow intercollege contact if both parties agreed.

Somehow, Zuckerberg and Moskovitz managed their course loads at Harvard while working feverishly to keep Thefacebook running. Zuckerberg hired another friend, high school classmate and Caltech student Adam D'Angelo, to help Moskovitz with the expansion. Although the project still hadn't earned them any money, Saverin submitted the paperwork to register Thefacebook as a business. The potential for earning was certainly there; investors were already offering to buy Thefacebook. Zuckerberg even turned down an offer of $10 million.[10] He wasn't ready to give up control of his project.

CHAPTER **THREE**

FACEBOOK TAKES ON THE WORLD

As the summer of 2004 drew near, Palo Alto, California, called to Zuckerberg. He had several friends who planned to live in the area. Palo Alto was a haven of technology. When he left for California, Zuckerberg didn't know he would not return to Harvard. He also wasn't sure Thefacebook would survive, despite its impressive success up to that point. He and Harvard classmate Andrew McCollum were already working on a new project, Wirehog. This program would let users share music, video, and text files. They planned to blend it into Thefacebook.

Zuckerberg rented a house for himself and team members willing to join him. Soon after, young businessman Sean Parker joined

Palo Alto has long been a hotbed of high-tech start-up companies.

FACEBOOK COMPANY CULTURE

Zuckerberg's uniform hasn't changed since college. A T-shirt with hoodie and jeans is his usual work outfit. One exception was when he wore a tie to work throughout 2009 to emphasize the serious times for the company. Zuckerberg is unfazed whether being interviewed or meeting with a major investor, and dressing to impress is not his style. "I really want to clear my life to make it so that I have to make as few decisions as possible about anything except how to best serve [Facebook's] community," he explains.[1]

As Facebook grew, Zuckerberg simplified employees' lives by offering many comforts at work, including free food and a laundry service. This helps relieve the pressure of long and focused work. Employees work in teams. Everyone contributes, regardless of job title or background. This culture is designed to help employees grow, learn, and experiment.

them. Parker had been the cofounder of Napster, an online music-sharing service that had upended the music industry in the late 1990s and early 2000s. Parker called on a lawyer to help turn Thefacebook into a company with contracts, a payroll, and everything else a functioning business needs. Zuckerberg and the other programmers focused on improving Thefacebook's computer infrastructure so it could handle its increasing number of users. They were still opening to more schools, even through the summer. They expected even more users when fall rolled around and new first-year students registered with the service.

FACING THE FINANCIAL NEEDS

Thanks to the company's use of free software and databases, Thefacebook needed little money at the start. But making sure that the system could handle the load required new and expensive servers. Saverin contacted an ad firm, Y2M, about placing clients' ads on the site. Y2M interested credit card company MasterCard in advertising. The company began cautiously, only planning to pay Thefacebook when students applied for credit cards. But David Kirkpatrick, author of *The Facebook Effect,* an account of the company's history, reports that "within one day [MasterCard] received twice the [credit card] applicants it had expected for the entire four-month campaign."[2] Saverin's efforts led to much-needed funds. The ad company also wanted to invest. Once again, Zuckerberg turned the company down, this time by making his price too high.

But Parker continued talking with investors. Parker's handling of business arrangements annoyed Saverin, who felt he had been chosen for the role. Since Saverin controlled the bank account, he threatened to withhold payments until his role was made clear. But, despite enlisting Y2M, Saverin's business skills had not impressed Zuckerberg or the team, and he hadn't joined them in Palo Alto. Zuckerberg had asked Saverin to create a business model, organize the company over the summer, and seek funding. These tasks hadn't been completed, so Zuckerberg turned them over to Parker. By September, Zuckerberg was calling Parker the company president, and he squeezed Saverin out of the company. In response, Saverin started a lawsuit. Zuckerberg settled it by retaining Saverin's name as an official company cofounder and paying him a settlement.

Toward the end of the summer, Zuckerberg had made another important decision. He would not return

Saverin played an important role in Facebook's early days.

to Harvard. Instead, he would devote all his time to Thefacebook—and to Wirehog. Moskovitz, Parker, and a couple of others stayed with him. By fall, the number of Thefacebook members had increased to 200,000.[3] The company's finances were strained. Then Zuckerberg met Peter Thiel, former CEO of PayPal and a major technology investor. Thiel invested $500,000 in the company.[4] Their money issues were solved—for the moment.

However, expenses continued to rise, and Zuckerberg realized that Facebook needed more money. Y2M led the company to advertising deals with Paramount Pictures and Apple. Gradually, necessity forced Zuckerberg to let go of his reluctance to advertise. Although the company

THE SOCIAL NETWORK

The award-winning 2010 movie *The Social Network* depicted the early years of Facebook, including Zuckerberg's conflicts with the Winklevoss twins and Saverin. It was based on Ben Mezrich's book *The Accidental Billionaires*. The book, Mezrich admitted, is a "dramatic narrative account," made from interviewees' memories along with factual documents.[5] This is important, says Mark Harris in his article "Inventing Facebook," because Mezrich follows Saverin's version of events. The film's screenwriter, Aaron Sorkin, did his own research and shows various other views. Still, Harris points out that Sorkin wrote the Zuckerberg character with traits that "represent a big leap of imagination."[6] However, author David Kirkpatrick feels the movie, which suggests Zuckerberg developed Facemash and later Facebook with the intention of impressing a girlfriend who turned him down, is "horrifically unfair."[7]

MYSPACE

The social networking site Myspace bloomed in 2003 after Friendster's failure. It grew quickly. By 2007, it had 70 million users in the United States.[8] That made it the country's most popular social network. In addition, users spent more time there than on similar sites. They liked the ability to design the look of their personal page. Unlike with Facebook, where users had to use their real names, users could open accounts with any name they chose.

However, hiding behind false names led to bullying and even violence against users. The site soon took on sexual overtones, with users posting suggestive pictures of themselves. Sometimes predators chatted with and met underage users. Reports of such crimes were rampant. They led one observer to create a blog, MyCrimeSpace, which reported crimes enabled by Myspace.

Facebook passed Myspace in user count in 2009. Myspace continued a steady decline in the years to come. In 2018, Myspace still existed, though it had shifted its focus to music and entertainment industry news.

would accept more investors, advertising would become Facebook's main source of income.

Meanwhile, Myspace loomed as a major competitor. The social networking site, launched in 2003, was more popular than Thefacebook. Many users visited the site several times a day. One reason for Myspace's success was that it allowed users to sign on at age 14. (It began with a requirement that users be 16 years old, but, with countless younger users signing on anyway, it lowered the age to 14.) Without a way to verify age, children under 14 logged on as well. Thefacebook was still limited to college students. Zuckerberg had been watching

FACEBOOK'S INCOME[9]

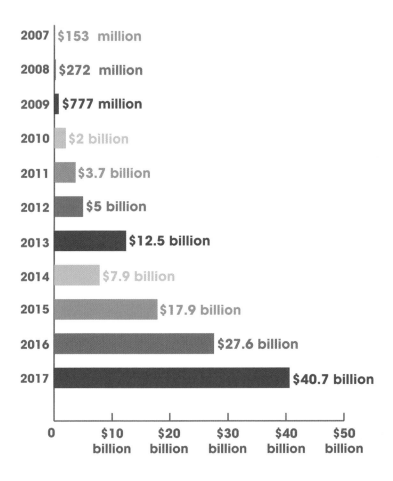

Year	Income
2007	$153 million
2008	$272 million
2009	$777 million
2010	$2 billion
2011	$3.7 billion
2012	$5 billion
2013	$12.5 billion
2014	$7.9 billion
2015	$17.9 billion
2016	$27.6 billion
2017	$40.7 billion

Selling advertising that would be displayed to Facebook's rapidly growing user base led to skyrocketing revenues for the company.

Myspace for some time. To reach his goals, Thefacebook needed to beat Myspace.

FACEBOOK'S FAST RISE

Thefacebook continued expanding in 2005. It became available to more colleges, and then to all US colleges. In September, it dropped the word *the* from its name after purchasing the www.facebook.com domain for $200,000.[10] Facebook also opened up registration to US high school students. Soon Facebook averaged 20,000 new members each day.[11] Finally, in September 2006, the company allowed anyone with an email address to join the site and make an account.

In October 2007, Microsoft invested $240 million in Facebook. From its initial team of college suitemates, Facebook planned to expand to 700 employees that year.[12] The number of active Facebook users rose to more than 70 million by the next year.[13] New chief operating officer Sheryl Sandberg joined the company in 2008 with the goal of boosting Facebook's growth and income. Facebook passed Myspace's number of users in May 2009, becoming the most popular social network in the United States.

SHERYL SANDBERG

Facebook hired Sheryl Sandberg as its chief operating officer (COO) in 2008. Sandberg had been a vice president at Google, handling global online sales and operations. She built successful advertising programs that helped push Google's income higher than ever before. Her 2013 book *Lean In*, which advised women on succeeding in business, drew national attention.

Zuckerberg hired Sandberg to guide Facebook's foreign expansion. She was also charged with directing marketing, human resources, and the privacy departments. In other words, she would have much to do with how people saw the company—and with ensuring its financial success. Despite Facebook's popularity, the company was losing money when Sandberg came on board. Sandberg was especially attracted to Facebook, she said, because "the opportunity to help another young company to grow into a global leader is the opportunity of a lifetime."[14] By focusing on recruiting small businesses to advertise on the website, Sandberg turned Facebook's finances around. Among the support Facebook now offers businesses are courses in ten languages to help them create ads on mobile devices.

Sandberg has been ranked by *Fortune* magazine as one of the most powerful women in business.

CHAPTER **FOUR**

NEW FEATURES

Facebook's array of features grew quickly. One early and popular feature was the Wall, a public bulletin board on users' profiles. Users loved the opportunity to comment and post photos on their friends' profiles.

It worked well for Facebook, too. With users checking their own and each other's Walls for new posts, Zuckerberg and his team began talking about a sort of "trance" that took hold of users. As Parker explained, "It was hypnotic. You'd just keep clicking and clicking and clicking from profile to profile, viewing the data."[1] Facebook began targeting ads to users based on data from their profiles, such as where they lived and what bands they liked. Time spent on the site was as important to Facebook as the number of users. The greater the time, the greater the contact with ads. The Wall became Timeline in 2012.

A central part of using Facebook has always been customizing the profile page to reflect the user's personality.

Another feature was forming groups. Users could set up pages for groups. A group's page had the same information and features that were available to individual users. It was a natural fit for clubs and political groups. Silly groups formed at the start, such as the "I hate the guy my thesis is about" group.[2] Today, celebrity fan groups are among the most popular Facebook groups.

NEWS FEED AND FACEBOOK CONNECT HELP ADVERTISERS

One of the most controversial features was the News Feed, introduced in 2006. It showed users a list of their friends' activities on Facebook—what groups they joined, what photos they posted, and what public messages they sent. Before this, only a visit to a user's page would reveal such activity. Now, posts became much more public by default.

Many users felt News Feed invaded their privacy, so Facebook gave them more control over the kinds of posts they would see. Soon, ads popped up in the News Feed too. A gray tag showed that the messages were not from friends. When companies on Facebook posted updates, these messages would go to those who had become "fans" and customers. Facebook Connect, a feature launched in 2008, let users log in to other sites using their Facebook

Zuckerberg often introduces major Facebook design changes onstage at Facebook's F8 conferences.

username and password, connecting the account to their Facebook profile. It fed online activity back to Facebook, where that information could be posted to friends' News Feeds. "Who wants to broadcast the news that he's bought a can of Sprite? And who wants to see that on a News Feed?" asks Steven Levy in his *Newsweek* article "Do Real Friends Share Ads?"[3]

FROM CHAT TO MESSENGER

In April 2008, Facebook introduced Chat, an instant messaging program. Two years later, a flaw in the system allowed users to see their friends' private chats and friend requests. Users were alarmed. Facebook responded quickly by repairing the program. It also added a video option to Chat called Facebook Live. Then Facebook struck a deal with a competitive instant messaging program, AOL Instant Messenger (AIM), to allow its millions of users to interact with their friends on Facebook.

Chat soon became available on cell phones. In 2016, Facebook switched its users from the Chat app to a new app called Messenger. Messenger is a stand-alone product, meaning a user doesn't have to go through Facebook. It also means those who don't have Facebook accounts can use it. Messenger rose to more than 1.3 billion users in September 2017.[6] That made it one of Facebook's most popular apps, second only to the messaging service WhatsApp, which Facebook bought in 2014. WhatsApp is enormously popular outside the United States. It was the most popular messaging service in 104 countries in 2017. Zuckerberg later noted that 1.5 billion users send 60 billion messages every day via WhatsApp.[7]

LIKING FACEBOOK

Facebook acquired the online sharing service FriendFeed in 2009. The two companies had some features in common, such as a real-time feed of friends' activity. Facebook's programmers integrated some of FriendFeed's most popular features into their own service. One of these was the Like button. With it, users

WHATSAPP OR MESSENGER?

Since Facebook owns both WhatsApp and Messenger, it isn't surprising that the two services offer most of the same features. Both free apps focus on sending text, photos, and videos to other users. Users can even cluster a small group of photos and videos to create a picture story. They can also chat with audio and video for free. Messenger has animations to liven up chats. It also offers special effects and filters for photos. WhatsApp also has a few filters and emojis overlaid on photos. Users can draw or add text to them, but aside from those few options, this app isn't as playful. The simpler approach may be what gives WhatsApp the edge overseas. It uses less data to run than Messenger, and so it is preferable in places where mobile bandwidth is more expensive or where there are smaller data caps.

can indicate that they like a post, photo, or other piece of content, and they share it with online friends. They can also show that they like an organization or business. Companies clamored for users to hit Like. This makes it possible for that company to target ads to those users. Because the Like is displayed to users' friends, it creates yet another advertisement.

A lawsuit filed in 2010 argued that teens should have their parents' permission to use the Like button because the minors' names and pictures were used to sell products. Facebook contested the lawsuit, and it was settled in 2013. The court allowed the practice as long as Facebook included in its terms of service that those under 18 must state that they have their parents' consent for their pictures to appear in ads.

Facebook offers no Dislike button. Zuckerberg explains, "We don't want to turn Facebook into a forum where people are voting up or down on people's posts. That doesn't seem like the kind of community we want to create." Barbara Speed, a writer for the *New Statesman,* thinks it has more to do with keeping the traffic running on Facebook. "Negative feedback drives users away," she argues. "A 'dislike' button could slow the never-ending

Businesses often encourage customers to click the Like button on the business's Facebook page.

stream of News Feed content down to a trickle—and that, after all, is Facebook's worst nightmare."[8]

INSTAGRAM

With 500 million users by July 2010, Facebook was the clear world leader in online social networking. Zuckerberg thought he saw a rival in the recently created photo-sharing site Instagram. In 2012, Facebook purchased it for $1 billion. Facebook usually acquires small businesses, but Instagram had about 30 million users at the time of purchase.[9]

Instagram was to retain much of its independence. "We need to be mindful about keeping and building on Instagram's strengths and features rather than just trying to integrate everything into Facebook," Zuckerberg explained. Facebook friends would not automatically have access to Instagram posts. Instagram would also keep up its relationships with competing social networks. "At the same time," Zuckerberg added, "we will try to help Instagram continue to grow by using Facebook's strong engineering team and infrastructure."[10]

Instagram describes itself as "a fast, beautiful and fun way to share your life with friends and family." It invites users to "take a picture or video, choose a filter to transform its look . . . then post to Instagram."[11] By January 2018, Instagram had reached 500 million daily users.[12]

Features Timeline

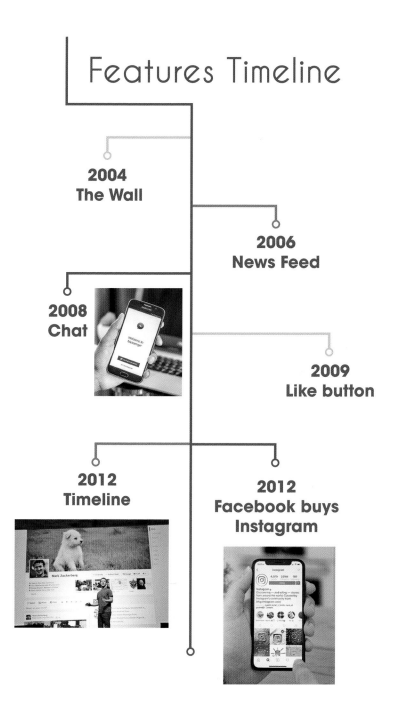

2004
The Wall

2006
News Feed

2008
Chat

2009
Like button

2012
Timeline

2012
Facebook buys Instagram

CHAPTER **FIVE**

FACEBOOK AND FRIENDSHIP

L ike many first-year college students, Allison Scott was nervous about going to Duke University for the Fall 2005 semester. It isn't easy to start over in a new, larger place, knowing no one. That's where Facebook came in. "It made us a lot more secure before coming to college," she said. "Having a lot of friends before coming to school makes you a lot more confident once you get here."[1]

Since its beginning, Facebook has been all about finding and communicating with friends, and later, family. Scott prepared that summer by connecting with nearly 400 other students. But she was in for a surprise. "Once I got here, it was just too hard and too awkward to walk up to people and say, 'I know you from the facebook.'" She cut her list to 228 and then added people she met face-to-face.[2]

Facebook is a popular tool for connecting with people on college campuses.

Others have had the same experience. Some stated that they felt "stalked" when someone known to them only online appeared in the flesh. They may also feel embarrassed that people who feel like strangers can see their personal posts online.

FRIEND CRAZY

Another problem is that many people feel obsessed with collecting online friends. In *The Facebook Effect*, Kirkpatrick notes that "friending"—adding Facebook friends—"had an element of competitiveness from day one. . . . If your roommate had 300 friends and you only had 100, you resolved to do better." Student Susan Gordon received emails from real-life friends as soon as Thefacebook hit Dartmouth College. They urged her to start friending, or else "she would be way behind" when they returned to school.[4]

Many internet sites suggest ways to quickly grow Facebook friend lists. Sometimes strangers even offer to promote other users. Facebook's friend limit is 5,000. Some object to that as random and confining if they are near or at that limit. Facebook requires that businesses, public figures, and organizations—who are likely to exceed the limit—open special pages that are linked to their personal accounts.

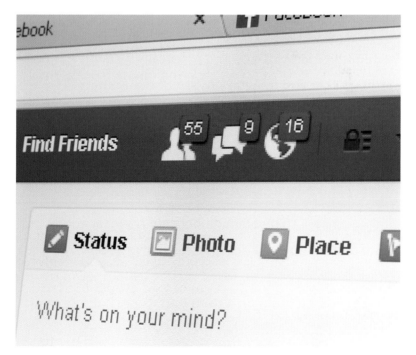

Accumulating long friend lists can become an unhealthy obsession.

Kirkpatrick observes, "Though many people do not use it this way, [Facebook] has always been explicitly conceived and engineered . . . as a tool to enhance your relationships with the people you know in the flesh—your real-world friends, acquaintances, classmates, or co-workers."[5]

The push for lengthy friend lists is often driven by the desire to seem popular. Researcher Graham G. Scott reports in his article "More than Friends" that being seen as popular doesn't rest simply on the friend tally. The Timeline action and number of photos also figure in. If these factors suggest a user is popular, Scott notes they "were rated more socially and physically attractive, more approachable and more extroverted" than others.[6] His study was based largely on feedback from active young adult Facebook users.

TOO MANY FRIENDS?

When users ask that someone become their Facebook friend and that person accepts, they have access to each other's Timeline and friends. If they reach out, even by liking or commenting on a third party's post, they can—if both agree—expand their friend list exponentially. But "after a point," argues Scott, "less is more in terms of number of online friendships."[7] Some feel the ideal number of friends is around 300. Any more and others may feel the user is padding the list to impress.

However, 300 may be twice as many as people need. University of Oxford professor Robin Dunbar looked at the online friends issue and pointed out that "our social worlds are actually very small. . . . The reason is simple. Our brains aren't big enough to allow us to have deeply meaningful relationships with more than a handful of people." He estimates the maximum number of meaningful friendships a person can have to be about 150, with only five very close relationships. Family members are among the circle of people's friendships. Members of large families with close ties often have fewer close friends outside the family. "Yes, we can list 1,000 names on our social network site," Dunbar explains, "but names is precisely all they are. . . . In real

LONELY CONNECTIONS

"Where we want to be cautious . . . is when the sound of a voice or a cup of coffee with a friend is replaced with 'likes' on a post," suggests Holly Shakya. Shakya, a University of California professor, studied the health of long-term Facebook users.[8]

The problem goes beyond replacing time together, says social psychologist Sherry Turkle. Social media also allows people to be elsewhere with others. Turkle gives the example of a teen party. When awkward moments come up, teens may feel like leaving. Instead of learning to work through it, teens often stare at their phones and use social media. They have "left" the party while there.

life, we gain signals about an individual's true feelings and honesty from a touch that we simply cannot replicate virtually on the internet."[9]

DOES SOCIAL MEDIA EQUAL SOCIAL ISOLATION?

Researchers Jean M. Twenge, Gabrielle N. Martin, and W. Keith Campbell found that teens' happiness, self-esteem, and life satisfaction dropped after 2012. This time, they note, was when smartphones became popular. This doesn't mean all social media use is damaging, cautions their report, published in the journal *Emotion* in 2018. "It's very difficult to carry on friendships in high school these days without texting at all or being on social media," Twenge says.[10] But teens who limit their use, so they spend more time in other activities, are happier. In other words, face-to-face time, reading print media, and even doing homework all led to greater happiness. The researchers also found that more screen time leads to less and poorer sleep. This can cause teens to be unhappy and do poorly in school and elsewhere. Teens who spend six hours or more a day looking at screens are "about twice as likely to be unhappy than those spending only a few hours a week," the report states.[11]

Researchers led by Brian Primack found another reason for the unhappiness. The researchers studied isolation and social media use among young adults. They found that greater social media use tends to go with feeling alone. It's a chicken-and-egg sort of issue, they say—it's not clear which one causes the other, or whether there is any direct causation at all. Those who feel isolated already may seek online contact more often. Or using the media too much may increase feelings of isolation.

TECH EXPERTS WORRY ABOUT EFFECTS

In February 2018, former Facebook and Google workers joined forces to form the Center for Humane Technology. These tech experts "are worried about the effects of unchecked tech use and social media on children," writes Alix Langone in a *Time* article. "The largest supercomputers in the world are inside of two companies— Google and Facebook," says cofounder Tristan Harris, "and where are we pointing them? We're pointing them at people's brains, at children." One of the center's first efforts is a campaign called "The Truth about Tech." It plans to take the educational campaign to 55,000 schools to make students and others aware of problems with overusing online technology.[12]

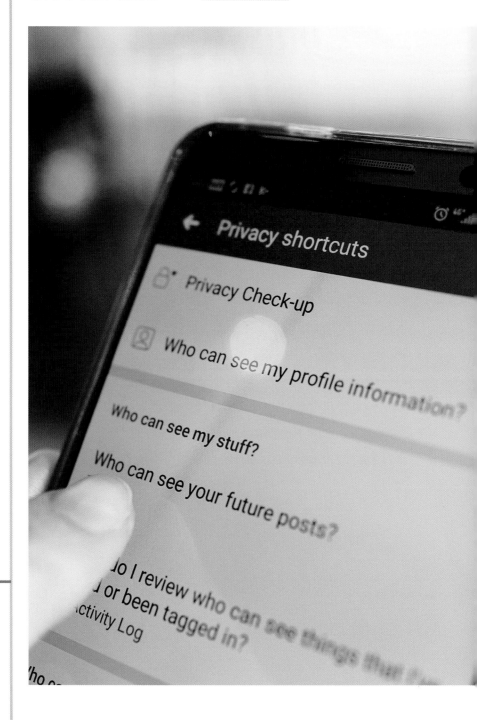

CHAPTER SIX

PRIVACY AND SHARING

Loss of privacy has been an issue for Facebook—and social media generally—since almost the beginning. Facebook involves an odd blurring of private and personal, observe Graham Meikle and Sherman Young in their book *Media Convergence*. As users type away, alone in a room or alone in a crowd, it feels like a solo activity. It feels private. That feeling of privacy sometimes prompts users to reveal things more personal than they would normally share in public.

When a message appears on their News Feed, it can also be hard to tell the difference between a personal and a public message. It is broadcast, Meikle and Young argue, the same way a television program is, for anyone who might be looking on. This is part of what makes "Facebook . . . so fascinating," they say. "It mixes

Facebook's privacy settings are designed to let users control what information friends and strangers can see.

up the personal message with the message sent to nobody in particular."[1]

Most people naturally shift behavior, speech, and level of formality depending on whom they are with. They act one way with a close friend, another way with a teacher or boss, and yet another way with a parent. Zuckerberg has a different feeling. He has said, "The days of you having a different image" for the different people in your life "are probably coming to an end pretty quickly. . . . Having two identities for yourself is an example of a lack of integrity."[2]

The blurring of the lines between public and private personas has created new problems in society. Many teens and adults have had to learn that the hard way. In a 2017 Kaplan Test Prep survey of more than 350 US college admissions officers, 35 percent said they looked at students' social media profiles to help them decide whether to accept a student. Nearly half of these officers, 47 percent, said they had found positive information about the student. There was one, for example, who founded a business with her mother. Another had posted a photo of herself receiving a school award. Conversely, 42 percent of the officers found posts that discouraged them from admitting the student. Among these were signs of racism, criminal actions, and pictures of the student with weapons. Kaplan's executive director of research, Yariv Alpher, summed up the issue this way: "College applicants need to be aware of what others can find about them on social networks and make sure it reflects well on them. For better or worse, social media has become an established factor in college admissions, and it's more important than ever for applicants to make wise decisions."[3]

Facebook postings can create job problems, too. Kirsten, a 22-year-old waitress, complained on Facebook about getting poor tips at work. Her post offended a Facebook friend, who told the restaurant's manager. Kirsten was fired. Like admissions officers, employers search online to learn about job applicants. Social media specialist Dan Schawbel observes, "A Google search of your name is the new handshake. People are already

Sarah Ball, a victim of cyberbullying during high school, later helped mentor young victims of cyberbullying.

searching for you online even before you meet them." College student Emma, 20, adds, "Your tweets and your Facebook posts . . . [are] out there permanently . . . for everyone to see."[4]

CYBERBULLYING

Among those negative posts are all-too-common instances of cyberbullying. A common scenario is what many call revenge porn. Most often, the victim is female. While in an intimate relationship, she sends her partner a revealing picture of herself. When the couple breaks up, she finds he has posted it on Facebook for all to see. Many embarrassed and harassed victims feel their lives have been ruined. Some commit suicide.

Other times people are subjected to the same kind of bullying found in schoolyards and workplaces. Being online, however, magnifies it. Several things tend to make cyberbullying more brutal, points out Kimberly Miller in her article "Cyberbullying and Its Consequences." For one thing, these bullies don't have to face the victim in public, where others may object or step in. Cyberbullies are also protected from their victims' reactions, which may provoke guilt. These factors tend to make cyberbullies

FACEBOOK'S RESPONSE TO POSTED ABUSE

"Facebook receives tens of thousands of potential 'sextortion' and 'revenge porn' cases a month," reveals Cara McGoogan in a 2017 article for London's *Daily Telegraph*. Her information came from "leaked company documents." Of nearly 54,000 cases reported, only 14,130 accounts were taken down. There is no way to know how many other such posts have not been reported. McGoogan notes that the documents also say that "Facebook will not delete videos and images depicting violence, self-harm, and child abuse of a nonsexual nature." Facebook's reasoning is that the posts may help "draw attention to mental illness or be newsworthy."[5] At the time the article was written, Facebook had decided to ban posts involving abuse of the disabled or those with major health problems.

bolder. For the victim, it seems that there is no escape. Prior to social media, someone taunted at school found refuge, at least, at home. Today, the bullying is on the victim's phone and computer screen. The attacks can come "at all times of the day," Miller states. What's more, someone "spreading a vicious rumor" can broadcast it to an entire school or community instantly using social media.[6]

STARS AND BAD ACTORS

Sometimes, the amount and type of sharing goes to extremes. Many have suggested that Facebook is a playground for narcissists— those who think a little too highly of themselves. With lots of photos, updates detailing daily events, and so on, some seek to grab the notice of the masses. College senior Namwan Leavell calls it by another oft-used name: exhibitionism. Thinking of individuals and couples who plaster their Timelines with photos and notes about their activities, Leavell says, "It's all part of the 'my life is so great' dog-and-pony show of social media." Nothing is wrong with sharing, she feels, but posting "every waking moment" of a couple's life turns "a relationship into an online brand."[7]

Some posts may depict things that are banned by Facebook's terms of service, such as violent content. In 2015, London's *Daily Mirror* reported on a video of teenage boys fighting bare-handed. Within two days of being uploaded, the video had already won thousands of likes. Facebook shut down the video, but one user bragged that he or she would be taking the video elsewhere. Similar fight-related pages continue to pop up on Facebook. "It may be impossible to remove all traces of embarrassing, inaccurate, or sensitive information," Dennis O'Reilly reminds readers in a *CNET* article. "As the saying goes, 'online is forever.'"[8]

Users may make confessions or cries for help on social media. For example, singer Sinead O'Connor published a video revealing that she was suicidal and living in a New Jersey motel. Facebook has offered means for stopping suicides. The company works with several suicide

Facebook employs people to manually review content that is flagged as inappropriate.

prevention organizations to create a series of suggestions. Those who find someone expressing suicidal ideas can report it to Facebook and get advice on offering support. Facebook teams worldwide review such reports. Recently, Facebook added artificial intelligence to help report potential suicides.

Getting rid of graphic violence and other disturbing content can be harder. The company has policies against such material, especially when it depicts people under 18. But it's a balancing act with free speech rights.

And keeping up with such posts is an endless task for the people whose job it is to review them. With up to 8,000 posts daily to review, former moderators say that they had just moments to decide whether each post met Facebook's standards. The material they must review can be so disturbing that Facebook offers its moderators counseling.

CHAPTER SEVEN

A TOOL FOR SOCIAL CHANGE

S tarting in late 2010 and moving into the next year, young people in the Middle East and northern Africa launched a series of uprisings known as the Arab Spring. "They are the Internet Generation . . . or the Facebook Generation . . . or just call them the Miracle Generation," exclaimed Professor Hassan Nafaa of Egypt's Cairo University.[1] They were protesting oppressive leaders and their lack of free elections. Unemployment, poverty, high food costs, and other social problems also prompted the movement. Discontent had been growing for a long time.

The protests began in Tunisia. Under the rule of president Zine al-Abidine Ben Ali, people dared not complain very loudly. The online group Takriz, safe in its anonymity, had been speaking out since 1998. Its first demands were for free

Protesters in many countries, including Yemen, used Facebook as a tool to coordinate their actions.

speech and lower internet costs. Internet censorship was severe under Ben Ali. The country had less internet freedom than Iran and China, two countries notorious for their censorship, reports Rebecca J. Rosen in an article for the *Atlantic*. Protesters used many internet tools, but a Takriz cofounder called Facebook "the GPS for this revolution."[2] Takriz published cases of police brutality and other abuses. Others began to see that they were not the only ones unhappy with conditions. Each online comment grew a little braver. Then, in late 2010, a police officer ordered a vendor to give up his unregistered vegetable cart. The upset vendor set himself on fire, becoming a martyr to the cause. By then, Facebook had more than one million Tunisian members,

MUZZLING FACEBOOK

Several countries have blocked their citizens from access to Facebook and other sites. Usually they do it to prevent statements against the government and to make it harder to organize protests. The list of these countries changes, but China and Iran have long been among them. Another tactic governments have tried is scanning posts for citizens who oppose the government. They search for key words that seem to conflict with Facebook's Community Standards and complain to the company. The Community Standards include rules against hate speech, crime, and violence. If publicly disagreeing with the government is illegal, the poster is engaging in crime. Facebook then removes the user's account and the user has no way to fight it or to find out who objected to the post. Meanwhile, the government is free to post its own propaganda online.

the news company Al Jazeera America reported. News of the vendor's death spread. Protests in the streets began. They were videotaped and posted online. Oppressed people in other nations took notice. The protests spread to a dozen countries.

Governments were toppled, and some positive changes happened. However, the changes didn't lead to new freedom and prosperity overall. New leadership was often shaky. In some instances, extremist groups swept in to take advantage of the chaos. In a report three years after the events started, the British Broadcasting Corporation (BBC) suggested that while Facebook may have helped spread the word, Western media may have overstated its role. In some of these countries, many cannot read or write and so rely on TV for news. Social media, the BBC says, "was confined largely to a well-educated and affluent . . . liberal elite."[3]

OCCUPY WALL STREET

Taking some cues from the Middle East, the New York–based Occupy Wall Street movement struck in late 2011. It was a leaderless movement that some people believed voiced unclear demands. At its heart, though, it protested the fact that those with the upper 1 percent of income had outsized influence and power in the United States. For that reason, it set its sights on the heart of the financial district in New York City.

The movement began with a July 2011 blog post by *Adbusters,* an activist magazine devoted to fighting commercialism. On its web page, *Adbusters* addressed "90,000 redeemers, rebels, and radicals," calling on them to #OCCUPYWALLSTREET. That September 17, the post continued, protesters should "set up tents, kitchens, peaceful barricades and occupy Wall Street for a few months."[4]

At first, the blog received little notice, but here and there people passed it on through the social media service Twitter. A Facebook page for the movement posted a clip of a protest on Wall Street on September 19. From there, it took off. By mid-October, reported the Reuters news service, there were 125 Occupy pages on Facebook.[5]

The police moved protesters from Wall Street but let them gather in nearby Zuccotti Park, whose owners also have strong ties to New York's financial district. There they remained for almost two months before police removed

Social media platforms gave Occupy Wall Street activists a way to spread their message across the country.

them. However, Occupy-aligned protests also took place across the United States and many other countries.

In his book *Social Media Freaks*, Dustin Kidd points out that activism conducted entirely online is limited. It's "click, like, share, move on," he says. Because people don't have to make real commitments to the cause, it's often called "slacktivism." But like the Arab Spring protests, he notes, "Occupy . . . found a way to merge occupation tactics with social media strategies."[6] The activists planned and spread the news on social media, but they staged protests in real life.

Occupy did not bring about radical change. But it did bring attention to inequality in the United States. When Vermont senator Bernie Sanders ran for the Democratic nomination for president in 2016, many of his campaign's themes echoed those of the Occupy movement. And several Occupy pages were still active on Facebook in 2018.

BLACK LIVES MATTER

The more recent Black Lives Matter movement also got a major push from Facebook. Many sources point to the 2012 Sanford, Florida, killing of 17-year-old Trayvon Martin as starting the movement. This indeed was the flash point, although African Americans in the United States had endured many generations of killings, torture, and other atrocities without hope of justice. Martin was returning from a trip to the store one evening. Volunteer neighborhood watchman George Zimmerman thought he looked suspicious and called police from his car. Police told him not to approach Martin. Zimmerman got out of his car anyway. He would later say Martin attacked him and that he shot the youth in self-defense. Martin was not armed.

When Zimmerman was found not guilty, African Americans and others were angry and frustrated. It seemed justice was still not available to African Americans. Californian Alicia Garza poured out her feelings in a long Facebook post, telling other African Americans that she loved them and that "black lives matter." A friend was so moved by her message that she shared it, using the hashtag #blacklivesmatter.

THE MILLION HOODIES MOVEMENT

On the night he was killed, Trayvon Martin was returning from a convenience store with an iced tea and candy. Like many teens, he wore a hooded sweatshirt—a hoodie—and was talking on his cell phone. Among the many protests that followed, aided by Facebook and other social media, the Million Hoodies Movement for Justice was started. Gathering 50,000 members, the organization works "to protect and empower young people of color from racial profiling and senseless gun violence through creative technology, strategic communications and grassroots power building."[8]

The movement was small until 2014, when several police shootings of unarmed black men hit the news. Researcher and activist Sam Sinyangwe collected data on police shootings following the death of Michael Brown, 18, of Saint Louis, Missouri. Sinyangwe found that African Americans "are three times more likely to be killed by police" compared with whites.[7] African Americans killed that year ranged from 12 to 65 in age. Criminology professor Lorie Fridell pointed to studies showing that people are affected by biases in deciding whether someone is a danger to them. All too often, people perceive black males as dangerous when they are not.

In July 2016, a Minnesota police officer pulled over Philando Castile to tell him his brake lights were out. Forty seconds later, the officer shot Castile five times. Castile had explained to the officer that he was legally carrying a gun. As he reached down, the officer began firing. The officer says he thought Castile was reaching for his gun. Castile and his passenger, Diamond Reynolds, said he was reaching for his license and registration, as the officer had asked. Once shots were fired, Reynolds began live streaming the events on Facebook. The video would later be shared throughout Facebook and shown on television and in court. The officer was eventually judged not guilty of murder, but he was let go from the police force.

Reynolds's live streaming of the event was an example of the citizen journalism now possible with tools like Facebook Live. Live streaming, says CNN's Brian Stelter,

Thanks in part to Facebook Live streaming, anger over the shooting of Philando Castile quickly spread and led to heated protests.

is "the newest form of citizen journalism—and the most immediate." Within days, Facebook users had seen Reynolds's video more than three million times.[9] Live streaming is a powerful tool that can offer important evidence and stir the public's feelings and actions, as it did with the Black Lives Matter movement.

HATE GROUPS

Hate groups also find their way to Facebook. While Zuckerberg sees the need for sharing diverse views, he says, "We've always taken down any post that promotes or celebrates hate crimes or acts of terrorism." In the same article that quoted Zuckerberg, CNN writer Heather Kelly noted that "Facebook deletes around 66,000 posts a week that it deems contain hate speech."[10] However, these groups persist. In 2016, the Southern Poverty Law Center named more than 200 hate groups on Facebook. Others worry, though, that limiting the speech of one group might lead to limiting free speech for all. David Snyder, executive director of the First Amendment Coalition, asks, "Do we the people really want private entities calling the

FACEBOOK'S ONE-SIDED NEWS

Many people get national and world news from Facebook. When newspapers were the preferred sources of information, readers were likely to see various points of view. But just as Facebook targets ads to specific users' preferences, so do preferences shape the news users receive. This limits their opportunities to consider other viewpoints. It can also sharpen the country's political divide. Writers Julia Carrie Wong, Sam Leven, and Olivia Solon asked five liberals to read Facebook's news for conservatives and five conservatives to read news intended for liberals. While it didn't affect everyone this way, for some, considering the other side's argument opened a window of understanding. In at least one case, it even changed a vote. "Maybe we should stop having social media," concluded a participant. "Maybe the ability with social media for people to construct their own reality to create a mob is not worth it."[11]

shots as to who can or can't participate in the discussion on the internet?"[12]

Even terrorists find ways to use the tools of social media. Their goal is not simply to strike terror in the hearts and minds of people they oppose. They also want to inspire others to follow them. That's where social media comes in. In 2016, a French extremist stabbed a policeman and the policeman's wife to death. While the couple's three-year-old looked on, the man recorded himself ranting on Facebook Live.

The Islamic State of Iraq and Syria (ISIS) and similar groups also use social media to radicalize and recruit new members. Imran Awan reports that Facebook and YouTube videos created by such groups often feature high production values and slick editing. Awan, who analyzed 100 radical Islamist Facebook pages, states that they portray "a glamorized and 'cool' image" and that "ISIS fighters are beginning to act as the new rock stars of global cyber jihad."[13]

CHAPTER EIGHT

"BUILDING THE WORLD WE ALL WANT"

Mark Zuckerberg wonders, "Are we building the world we all want?"[1] He has come a long way since his days of rating college students on their looks through Facemash. Facebook now has several projects that are explicitly designed to benefit society.

A social good initiative begun in 2013 is an early example—or at least social good was Facebook's stated intention. First called Internet.org and later renamed Free Basics, the plan was to offer free but limited internet service to those without it in underserved countries. Eighty-five percent of the world has cell phone coverage, notes Facebook. But with the high price of data connections and limited resources, many people do not connect to the internet

An initiative to provide free internet service is one of Facebook's major projects intended to make the internet more widely accessible.

and are deprived of its advantages. Facebook joined with telecom companies, nonprofits, and governments to provide internet access without data charges in Africa, Asia, and Latin America.

But criticism soon rose, and India even banned the venture. Facebook can easily overwhelm local companies, argues Sunil Abraham, India's director of the Centre for Internet and Society. Other critics point out that service is very limited, featuring just 150 websites and services per locality. It also emphasizes Western sites, meaning that popular local sites may be bypassed. Service in many common local languages is often not available. Olivia Solon, writing for the *Guardian*, says that Facebook sees the service as "an on-ramp" to paying for the full internet.[2] Meanwhile, Facebook gains more users and collects their data. Zuckerberg insists that Facebook is providing a valuable service, however, and continues the program.

Several initiatives that Facebook introduced more recently may be less controversial. In a February 2017 letter to Facebook users, Zuckerberg described history as a process of learning to "come together in ever greater numbers—from tribes to cities to nations." He's ready for Facebook to help move humanity toward a "global community."[3] To create this, communities develop five vital qualities. They must be supportive, safe, informed, civically engaged, and inclusive.

In November 2017, Facebook held its second annual Social Good Forum. Never short on ideas, Facebook revealed several new tools to work toward its lofty goal of giving "people the power to build a global community that works for all of us."[4]

SAFETY CHECK AND COMMUNITY HELP

After Japan's 2011 tsunami and earthquake, online newspaper reports included personal messages in live feed video and audio clips. The response to the tragedy inspired Facebook to create an app to help in crises. Called Safety Check, it was released in 2014. First, Facebook is notified

SOUND THE ALARM!

"The goal of Safety Check is to ensure people feel safe and connected during a crisis and not to create false alarm or panic," explained an unnamed Facebook spokesperson. But when Safety Check announced a "Violent Incident in Manhattan, New York," software engineer Hyman Rosen commented, "I thought it was remarkably silly."

In 2017, a truck driver mowed down people on a bike path, killing eight and injuring nearly 12 more. Rosen wasn't suggesting the event wasn't awful. Rather, he said, it caused undue panic. "Manhattan's got a few million people in it, and they're all going to go push buttons on Facebook saying I'm O.K.?" he asked.[5] Large numbers of the millions Facebook notified felt obligated to check in so family and friends wouldn't worry.

when crises occur. When it detects that many people are discussing the event, Safety Check activates. That allows users to let family and friends know that they are safe. Those receiving the message are invited to let others know they are OK.

In 2016, Facebook added Community Help to Safety Check. This feature lets people reach out to those in need in a crisis with offers of shelter, food, and so on. At the 2017 forum, Facebook announced that it would provide relief agencies such as the American Red Cross

Zuckerberg, *left*, met with Japanese prime minister Shinzo Abe to discuss the Safety Check feature in 2014.

and NetHope with the information gathered after natural disasters. In an article for the *Washington Post,* Hayley Tsukayama explains that the feature shows "how populations are moving, where they are checking in safely and how their normal routines have been disrupted." Facebook also provides "location density maps" to "show where people have fled to and when they are returning."[6] This data helps organizations learn where help is needed and what kind of assistance is needed. While Community Help isn't meant to respond to war and other man-made problems, that could be in its future.

FUNDRAISERS

Facebook has often been used to raise money for various causes using a tool on the site called Fundraisers. It provides donate buttons for live-streamed videos so viewers can respond right away. Earlier, Facebook charged charities 5 percent of the donations to

AUTOMATIC FUND-RAISERS

When natural disasters hit, Facebook is primed for action. Multiple mentions in News Feed trigger Facebook's crisis response pages. These encourage people to use the Safety Check and can also be used to ask for donations. A series of more than 20 fires in California in October 2017 were one such disaster. They destroyed some 8,400 buildings and killed at least 42 people.[7] It was the most destructive fire event the state had ever faced. Users reported personal stories and pictures from the disaster. Soon the donations rolled in.

cover confirming the charity and handling credit cards.[8] But a petition with 42,000 signatures convinced Facebook to drop the fee. The organization presenting the petition, the Syrian American Medical Society, said that it could treat thousands more people with the saved funds. Facebook has also pledged to donate up to $50 million yearly.[9] The funds are used to match donations to disaster relief and other crises. In 2017, Facebook announced that it was opening Fundraisers to more countries.

Fees still apply to Personal Fundraisers, Facebook's answer to crowdfunding site GoFundMe. However, Facebook's fees are a bit lower. This feature allows users to ask for help with school or health expenses or funds needed in a crisis.

BLOOD DONATIONS

Facebook has been in the blood business since 2008. At that time, it asked users for their blood type and notified them regularly about donating and as needs came up in their area.

In some countries, access to safe blood is limited, and family members may have to search for donors to help their loved ones. At the 2017 Social Good Forum,

Facebook announced it was expanding its blood donation program into new countries. The blood donation feature opened to India on October 1, 2017. By the November 29 forum, four million had signed up to donate. Facebook would soon add Bangladesh, said Naomi Gleit, vice president for social good: "[There,] like India, there are thousands of posts from people looking for blood donors every week."[10]

MENTORSHIP AND SUPPORT

The most exciting announcement, however, was the brand-new feature Mentorship and Support. The purpose of this feature, created by nonprofits, is to match

Social media can be used for getting the word out about blood donation.

those with a need with those who can help. Two new partnerships would kick off this new offering. The first is iMentor, an educational tool, which agreed to partner with Facebook. Begun in 1999, iMentor typically works with nonprofits to match a low-income student with a college graduate mentor for three to four years. Often the students have no role models for college success among family and friends. They may not have thought of college as an option for them. If they have, they may be bewildered by the application process. Once in college, these students may struggle and even drop out without someone to help them adjust to the challenges. The iMentor program provides this guidance. Now, iMentoring can begin on their Facebook pages.

Physicist Albert Einstein helped create the second partner, the International Rescue Committee (IRC). Einstein, who immigrated to the United States from Nazi Germany, brought together a group of American intellectual leaders in 1933. Two years earlier, an organization called the International Relief Association (IRA) had been formed in Europe to help "victims of civil oppression in many lands" regardless of their beliefs.[11] Einstein felt an American-based IRA could raise money to help other refugees who had fled from German dictator

The connections made possible by Facebook can be helpful for mentoring programs.

Adolf Hitler. A few years later, the IRA blended with another group under the name International Rescue Committee (IRC). Over its long history, the IRC would offer medicine, health care, childcare, and education to refugees from conflicts around the globe.

The IRC Facebook page helps educate people about refugees' problems and what IRC is doing to address them. It also raises funds and recruits volunteers to help refugees adjust to their new lives. Facebook expects the Mentorship and Support program may expand into areas such as career growth and fighting addiction.

FIXING FACEBOOK

As Facebook rolled out its social good programs, the American public had become sharply divided politically during the 2016 presidential campaign and election. As early as July 2016, the FBI began looking into Russian efforts to affect the US election. In September 2017, Facebook admitted to Congress that it had received $100,000 to run 3,000 political ads created by Russia.[1] In October 2017, representatives from Facebook and other social media companies testified before Congress on Russian attempts to influence the 2016 presidential election. They also discussed how the companies might block Russian meddling in future elections.

When January 2018 arrived, Zuckerberg admitted that the company had made "too many errors enforcing our policies and preventing

A large number of political ads displayed on Facebook and other social media platforms were linked to a Russian effort to sow divisions in the United States.

misuse of our tools."[2] Many people agreed. They wanted privacy and an end to "hacking, cyberbullying and social media scams," Lindsey Bever points out in a *Washington Post* article. "Facebook has a lot of work to do," Zuckerberg said, "whether it's protecting our community from abuse and hate, defending against interference by nation states, or making sure that time spent on Facebook is time well spent."[3]

Each year, Zuckerberg assigns himself a new challenge. One year it was to learn Mandarin Chinese, so he could talk with his wife's relatives. Another year it was to visit people in every state. In 2018, he announced, he would fix Facebook. Tackling Facebook's many problems is good. But some have greeted the news with the comment that he has simply decided to do his job this year.

FACEBOOK: RUSSIA'S TOOL OF CHOICE?

By mid-2018, details were still unraveling about Russia's actions during the election that brought President Trump to the White House. In March, the Department of Justice (DOJ) charged 13 Russians and three companies with plotting to affect voters. The DOJ's document details Russian efforts, citing Facebook and Instagram 41 times.

That is many times more than Twitter and YouTube were noted. Using stolen American identities, Russians are believed to have formed Facebook groups to discredit the Democratic candidate. They tried to divide people by posting ads and images spreading falsehoods. At least one ad told African Americans that neither candidate was worth their vote.

Facebook is not believed to have knowingly partnered with Russia. However, as Jonathan Albright, research director for Columbia University's digital journalism center, pointed out, "Facebook, essentially, gave them everything they needed." Facebook admitted that it sold political ads to the Russian front firm Internet Research Agency. Some of the ads were viewed by 150 million Americans.[4]

BRIDGING THE DIVIDE

The Russians' efforts to "muddy the waters" of American political debate deepened the divide between voters. The television show *60 Minutes* put together a 14-member group, half Trump supporters and half not, to discuss the issues. Some had never talked thoughtfully with the other side before. When *60 Minutes* learned that the group was still together six months later, contributor Oprah Winfrey visited them again. She learned that they started a private Facebook chat group to continue talking— every day. They also met in real time, doing things together and learning about each other's lives. Even though their positions did not change, they became friends. One of them explained, "now I'm looking at them as people, not as you're Trump or not Trump. This has been an incredible experience and an education for me."[5]

"How did Facebook, which prides itself on being able to process billions of data points," lamented Senator Al Franken in a Senate judiciary committee hearing, "not make the connection that electoral ads paid for in rubles were coming from Russia?"[6]

Colin Stretch, Facebook's vice president and general counsel, told the committee,

The foreign interference we saw is reprehensible and outrageous and opened a new battleground for our company, our industry, and our society. That foreign actors, hiding behind fake accounts, abused our platform and other Internet services to try to sow division and discord—and to try to undermine our election process— is an assault on democracy, and it violates all of our values.[7]

Stretch pointed out that Facebook has always reported suspicious activity to law enforcement. In October 2016, it deleted 5.8 million fake US accounts. It also canceled thousands of accounts before French and German elections. In 2018, Facebook decided to require more details from anyone posting election ads. They will have to reveal who is paying. In addition, Facebook is working on ways to check the identities of people creating

Stretch testified in front of Congress in November 2017.

Facebook pages. The company planned to hire more than 1,000 new employees to review ads.[8] The company is cooperating with the government's probes into Russian interference, and it is working with the FBI. It is also looking at its own methods to avoid being a pawn in a foreign country's schemes again.

CAMBRIDGE ANALYTICA AND THE #DELETEFACEBOOK MOVEMENT

In mid-March of 2018, newspapers broke a fresh story. Facebook had allowed a researcher at Cambridge Analytica, a British political consulting firm, to build a personality quiz for its users, available from 2013 through 2015. The quiz took advantage of a loophole in Facebook's system. It let the firm collect personal information from those who took it, as well as from the people on those users' friend lists. Cambridge Analytica helped Trump with his campaign. Both the company and the campaign claim that the firm did not use the Facebook data during the campaign. Others charge that it passed the data on to a public relations firm to craft political messages tailored to the voters whose data it had.

In an article for *Vox*, Alvin Chang wrote that it's possible that the firm's efforts didn't help Trump. "But," he argues, it "highlights a larger debate over how much users can trust Facebook with their data."[9] It is troubling, he adds, that Facebook knew about the data leak for more than two years before it owned up to it. *Vox* writer Aja Romano says that "Facebook expected its user data to be harvested."[10] In fact, Facebook stepped in to prevent such large-scale access to user data in 2015, after the damage was done. But as Romano points out, Facebook just hadn't foreseen anyone taking data from 50 million users. A few weeks later, Facebook admitted that Cambridge Analytica may have actually gathered the data of 87 million people, one million of them in the United Kingdom.[11]

Facebook responded with ads in several US and British newspapers just over a week after the scandal hit the news. "We have a responsibility to protect your information. If we can't, we don't deserve it," it proclaimed. Many feel the apology is too late. "The fallout [from the scandal] has been severe," writes Nick Statt for the *Verge*, "with numerous lawsuits, governmental inquiries, a #DeleteFacebook user boycott

"RUSSIAN WEAPONS TEST"

Since hijacked airliners slammed into the World Trade Center and the Pentagon on September 11, 2001, the date 9/11 has called up grim reminders for many Americans. It seemed eerie that on that date in 2014, people in Louisiana began receiving Facebook and Twitter messages about a chemical plant explosion. They said a toxic cloud would soon affect those in New Orleans and Baton Rouge. There was even a YouTube video claiming that the terrorist group ISIS had caused it.

There was no explosion and no toxic cloud. Russia wanted to see the effect of fake news on US citizens. It apparently liked the panic it saw. Next came the fake news about the election. "That was a Russian weapons test," Christopher Paul of the Rand Corporation, a think tank, explains.[12] The damage is more serious than causing panic, Paul explains. It causes people to distrust news sources and doubt facts.

Some users decided to stop using Facebook in light of what happened during the 2016 election season.

campaign, and a sharp drop in share price that's erased nearly $50 billion of the company's market cap."[13]

As for deleting Facebook accounts, it isn't as easy as users might think. Facebook urges them to "deactivate" instead, explains Alex Hern, a writer for the *Guardian*. That way, Facebook keeps their data. If users insist on deleting,

Facebook suggests that they may want to download their information first. That download can be a revelation to many who have never thought about all the information that Facebook stores. Users report that the data includes information about cell phone calls and text messages sent or received, contact data, calendar notes, and friends' birthdays.

Throughout March 2018 and into April, Facebook was a daily news item as its role in Russian election meddling and data mining of users continued to spill out. It seemed that the company's early motto, "Move fast and break things," had caught up with it. In 2014, Zuckerberg had introduced a new motto, "Move fast with stable infrastructure." It was not "as catchy," he admitted.[14] And apparently, Facebook didn't take the shift as far and as deeply as it should have.

After some attempts to hide its problems, Facebook stepped up to deal with them. But whether Facebook can fix itself is an open question. The same sort of data that Cambridge Analytica gleaned is what draws advertisers to Facebook. They depend on knowledge of users to target their ads. Without advertising, Facebook could not operate—at least not without charging users. There are no signs of Facebook backing off data collection. And its new feature that names users even in untagged photos seems to go in the opposite direction.

Sandy Parakilas, who oversaw policy and privacy at Facebook from 2011 to 2012, offers a proposal and warning. Parakilas recalls presenting a report on ways in which Facebook was ripe for privacy abuses. He even named those who might do it. He found senior staff unconcerned or even uninterested in news of election meddling. The company was, Parakilas reports, more concerned about "getting more users and making more money."[15] It wasn't until ten months after the election that Facebook owned up to its role in the problem. Tech companies can't be relied on to fix themselves, Parakilas advises. He says that legally mandated third parties must review instances of abuse and make sure that companies enforce their policies. Nearly half of policy infractions at Facebook were not correctly dealt with in 2017, he notes.

ZUCKERBERG GOES TO CONGRESS

In April 2018, Zuckerberg was called on to testify before both houses of Congress. Grilled for some ten hours with nearly 600 questions, he again took responsibility for

Zuckerberg's appearance before Congress drew intense media attention.

his company's mistakes. When Senator Richard Durbin asked him whether he'd care to share information such as where he was staying and whom he messaged publicly, Zuckerberg opted for privacy. "I think that may be what this is all about," the senator observed. "Your right to privacy."[16] Zuckerberg pledged again to fix Facebook's problems. Congress appeared to agree with Parakilas that government regulation might be needed.

By this time, *Business Insider* reported, about one out of every ten American users had quit Facebook. Seventeen percent removed the app from their phones. Thirty-five percent reduced their use.[17]

THINGS WILL BE BETTER— IN THREE YEARS

In early May 2018, Zuckerberg predicted that it would probably take three years to fix Facebook's major problems. The company began by keeping a closer watch on its apps to unearth problems such as unauthorized data collection. It also pledged to notify users when leaks occur. For the rest, though three years may seem too long, Zuckerberg's prediction may simply be realistic. "You can't just hire 30,000 people overnight to go do something," he explained. "You have to make sure that they're executing well and bring in the leadership and train them. And building up AI [artificial intelligence] tools—that's not something that you could just snap your fingers on either."[18]

Part of the challenge is restoring the company's reputation and winning back users. To that end, Facebook is running ads and continuing to work on new features. Many features were announced at its annual F8 conference beginning May 1, 2018. One example is FaceDate, a dating service. Facebook's still-large user base makes for an attractive pool of possibilities. "We've designed this with privacy and safety in mind from the beginning," Zuckerberg stated.[19] The new "Clear History"

Zuckerberg spoke at a technology convention in France in 2018 as part of his effort to rehabilitate Facebook's image after a series of scandals and controversies.

feature—similar to cleaning the browsing history from a web browser—was also designed to be reassuring for privacy-minded users. Instagram will have a new antibullying feature designed to filter out harassing comments. Users watched to see if Facebook would continue recovering from the #DeleteFacebook movement and increased skepticism about social media from the public. How well Facebook lives up to its promises and the government's response to current challenges may decide its future.

TIMELINE

2004
In February, Mark Zuckerberg releases Thefacebook at Harvard University; that summer, Zuckerberg moves to Palo Alto, California; by summer's end, Thefacebook receives several investments.

2005
Thefacebook becomes Facebook in September; Facebook creates a high school version.

2006
Facebook launches News Feed, which quickly draws massive protests about lack of privacy.

2007
In October, Microsoft invests $240 million in Facebook.

2009
In May, Facebook becomes the most popular social network in America, passing its rival, Myspace.

2010
The movie *The Social Network*, portraying Facebook's rise, is released.

2011
Facebook is used to help publicize and organize the Arab Spring, a series of protests against oppression in the Middle East.

2014
Facebook buys the messaging service WhatsApp.

2016

In July, Diamond Reynolds live streams the moments just after Philando Castile was shot by police; the video rivets the nation and is presented as evidence in court; it also energizes the Black Lives Matter movement.

2017

In February, Zuckerberg publishes a letter to users announcing a new goal for Facebook: working toward a "global community"; in September, Facebook tells Congress it had received $100,000 to run 3,000 political ads created by Russia during the 2016 presidential campaign; by the end of November, Facebook announces its new initiative, Mentorship and Support, at its second annual Social Good Forum.

2018

In January, Zuckerberg admits Facebook has made mistakes in several areas and pledges to focus on fixing Facebook within the year; in February, former Facebook and Google employees form the Center for Humane Technology to bring to light problems with online technology; in mid-March, the US Department of Justice charges 13 Russians and three companies with election meddling, citing Facebook as their primary tool; also in March, Facebook is accused of letting a political consulting firm, Cambridge Analytica, access the personal data of 50 million users to create messages tailored to them in support of Donald Trump.

ESSENTIAL **FACTS**

KEY PLAYERS

FOUNDER & CHIEF EXECUTIVE OFFICER (CEO)
- Mark Zuckerberg (from 2004)

CHIEF OPERATING OFFICER (COO)
- Sheryl Sandberg (from 2008)

KEY STATISTICS

- Thefacebook began with $1,000 each contributed by Zuckerberg and Eduardo Saverin, its first business manager.

- By 2007, 58 million people were actively using Facebook.

- In 2012, Facebook claimed 845 million members around the world.

- In 2017, Facebook's messaging service, Messenger, had 1.3 billion users.

- With 60 billion daily messages and 1.5 billion users, WhatsApp is the most popular messaging service.

- Five hundred million people use Instagram each day.

- Facebook had more than two billion users worldwide as of February 2018.

- Facebook admitted in 2018 that it failed to prevent Cambridge Analytica from accessing the information of 50 million users.

IMPACT ON HISTORY

Facebook has changed the way people relate to each other, with interaction occurring increasingly online instead of in person. It has blurred the line between private and personal and, with live streaming, popularized citizen journalism. The effects of these changes are still being studied by researchers.

QUOTE

"We have a responsibility to protect your information. If we can't, we don't deserve it."

—*Text of Facebook ad after Cambridge Analytica accessed personal information of 50 million users*

GLOSSARY

affluent
Well-off or wealthy.

anonymity
The state of having an unknown identity.

coalition
A collection of groups or people that have joined
together for a common purpose.

conversely
On the contrary; on the other hand.

discredit
To dishonor or hurt the reputation of someone
or something.

eerie
Weird; creepy; uncanny.

exponentially
At an increasing rate.

hacking
The use of a computer to gain unauthorized access
to another computer in order to view, copy, or
destroy data.

infraction
An action that breaks a rule or law.

marginalized
Excluded or treated as unimportant or of a lower class.

propaganda
Information that carries facts or details slanted to favor a single point of view or political bias.

replicate
To create a copy.

reprehensible
Disgraceful; objectionable; shameful.

ruble
The basic unit of Russian money.

thesis
Argument or main point; in college, a lengthy, final research paper written to earn a degree.

ADDITIONAL **RESOURCES**

SELECTED BIBLIOGRAPHY

Kardaras, Nicholas. *Glow Kids: How Screen Addiction Is Hijacking Our Kids—And How to Break the Trance*. Saint Martin's, 2016.

Kidd, Dustin. *Social Media Freaks*. Westview, 2017.

Kirkpatrick, David. *The Facebook Effect*. Simon & Schuster, 2010.

FURTHER READINGS

Eboch, M. M. *Big Data and Privacy Rights*. Abdo, 2017.

Harris, Ashley Rae. *Facebook: The Company and Its Founders*. Abdo, 2013.

ONLINE RESOURCES

Booklinks
NONFICTION NETWORK
FREE! ONLINE NONFICTION RESOURCES

To learn more about Facebook, visit **abdobooklinks.com**. These links are routinely monitored and updated to provide the most current information available.

MORE INFORMATION

For more information on this subject, contact or visit the following organizations:

CHILDNET INTERNATIONAL
Studio 14, Brockley Cross Business Centre
96 Endwell Road, London SE4 2PD
+44 (0)20 7639 6967
childnet.com/young-people/secondary
This organization is devoted to creating safety on the internet for kids of all ages. The Secondary page is aimed particularly at people ages 11 to 18.

FACEBOOK
1 Hacker Way
Menlo Park, CA 94025
650-543-4800
facebook.com/facebook
Facebook's headquarters is not open to visitors, but people can contact the company for information.

SOURCE NOTES

CHAPTER 1. ORGANIZING A MOVEMENT

1. Perry Stein. "The Woman Who Started the Women's March with Facebook Post Reflects." *Washington Post*, 31 Jan. 2017, washingtonpost.com. Accessed 21 Feb. 2018.

2. Erica Chenoweth and Jeremy Pressman. "This Is What We Learned by Counting the Women's Marches." *Washington Post*, 7 Feb. 2017, washingtonpost.com. Accessed 17 July 2018.

3. Aimee Blanchette. "Is Super Bowl Suggestion for the Birds?" *Star Tribune*, 16 Jan. 2018, startribune.com. Accessed 22 Feb. 2018.

4. Nina Agrawal. "How the Women's March Came into Being." *Los Angeles Times*, 21 Jan. 2017, latimes.com. Accessed 21 Feb. 2018.

5. Claire Stern. "An Afternoon with the Badass Women Behind the Women's March." *InStyle*, 17 Jan. 2017, instyle.com. Accessed 17 July 2018.

6. Perry Stein. "Women's March on Washington Planning for Big Crowds on Inauguration Weekend." *Washington Post*, 14 Nov. 2016, washingtonpost.com. Accessed 18 Mar. 2018.

7. Lorraine Boissoneault. "The Original Women's March on Washington and the Suffragists Who Paved the Way." *Smithsonian Magazine*, 23 Jan. 2017, smithsonianmag.com. Accessed 22 Feb. 2018.

8. Meredith Woerner. "Who Started the March? One Women." *Los Angeles Times*, 21 Jan. 2017, latimes.com. Accessed 22 Feb. 2018.

9. Christina Cauterucci. "The Women's March Was Just the Beginning." *Slate*, 17 Jan. 2018, slate.com. Accessed 24 Feb. 2018.

10. "Stats." *Facebook Newsroom*, 2018, newsroom.fb.com. Accessed 22 Feb. 2018.

11. "Bloomberg Billionaires Index." *Bloomberg*, 23 Feb. 2018, bloomberg.com. Accessed 23 Feb. 2018.

CHAPTER 2. THE BIRTH OF FACEBOOK

1. David Kirkpatrick. *The Facebook Effect*. Simon, 2010. 24.

2. Jose Antonio Vargas. "Mark Zuckerberg Opens Up." *New Yorker*, 20 Sept. 2010, newyorker.com. Accessed 28 Feb. 2018.

3. Kirkpatrick, *The Facebook Effect*, 26.

4. Kirkpatrick, *The Facebook Effect*, 27–28.

5. Kirkpatrick, *The Facebook Effect*, 30–31.

6. Kirkpatrick, *The Facebook Effect*, 32.

7. Kirkpatrick, *The Facebook Effect*, 35.

8. Tomio Geron. "Mark Zuckerberg: Don't Just Start a Company, Do Something Fundamental." *Forbes*, 20 Oct. 2012, forbes.com. Accessed 26 Feb. 2018.

9. Kirkpatrick, *The Facebook Effect*, 35.

10. Kirkpatrick, *The Facebook Effect*, 41.

CHAPTER 3. FACEBOOK TAKES ON THE WORLD

1. Deirdre Clemente. "Why American Workers Now Dress So Casually." *Atlantic*, 22 May 2017, theatlantic.com. Accessed 17 July 2018.

2. David Kirkpatrick. *The Facebook Effect*. Simon, 2010. 43.

3. Kirkpatrick, *The Facebook Effect*, 86.

4. Kirkpatrick, *The Facebook Effect*, 89–90.

5. Ben Mezrich. *The Accidental Billionaires*. Doubleday, 2009. 1.

6. Mark Harris. "Inventing Facebook." *New York*, 27 Sept. 2010, nymag.com. Accessed 17 July 2018.

7. David Kirkpatrick. "The Social Network: A Misleading View of Facebook's Birth." *Telegraph*, 14 Oct. 2010, telegraph.co.uk. Accessed 17 July 2018.

8. "Myspace Outperforms All Other Social Networking Sites." *BusinessWire*, 12 July 2007, businesswire.com. Accessed 17 July 2018.

9. "Investor Relations." *Facebook*, 2018, facebook.com. Accessed 17 July 2018.

10. Sarah Phillips. "A Brief History of Facebook." *Guardian*, 25 July 2007, theguardian.com. Accessed 17 July 2018.

11. Kirkpatrick, *The Facebook Effect*, 150.

12. "Microsoft Invests $240 Million in Facebook." *NBC News*, 24 Oct. 2007, nbcnews.com. Accessed 3 Mar. 2018.

13. Kirkpatrick, *The Facebook Effect*, 222, 225, 227.

14. Brad Stone and Miguel Helft. "Facebook Hires a Google Veteran, Sheryl Sandberg, as Its Chief." *New York Times*, 5 Mar. 2008, nytimes.com. Accessed 17 July 2018.

CHAPTER 4. NEW FEATURES

1. David Kirkpatrick. *The Facebook Effect*. Simon, 2010. 93.

2. Kirkpatrick, *The Facebook Effect*, 93.

3. Steven Levy. "Do Real Friends Share Ads?" *Newsweek*, 10 Dec. 2007, newsweek.com. Accessed 17 July 2018.

4. E. J. Westlake. "Friend Me If You Facebook." *TDR*, vol. 52, no. 4, 2008, 22.

5. "Facebook Founder Apologizes in Privacy Flap." *InformationWeek*, 8 Sept. 2006, informationweek.com. Accessed 17 July 2018.

6. Rani Molla. "WhatsApp Is Now Facebook's Second-Biggest Property, Followed by Messenger and Instagram." *Recode*, 1 Feb. 2018, recode.net. Accessed 7 Mar. 2018.

7. David Snelling. "WhatsApp vs. Facebook Messenger." *Express*, 18 Feb. 2018, express.co.uk. Accessed 7 Mar. 2018.

8. Barbara Speed. "'A Cursed Project': A Short History of the Facebook 'Like Button.'" *New Statesman*, 9 Oct. 2015, newstatesman.com. Accessed 7 Mar. 2018.

9. Evelyn M. Rusli. "Facebook Buys Instagram for $1 Billion." *New York Times*, 9 Apr. 2012, dealbook.nytimes.com. Accessed 3 May 2018.

10. Rusli, "Facebook Buys Instagram for $1 Billion."

11. "Instagram." *Facebook*, n.d., facebook.com. Accessed 7 Mar. 2018.

12. Salman Aslam. "Instagram by the Numbers." *Omnicore*, 1 Jan. 2018, omnicoreagency.com. Accessed 3 Mar. 2018.

CHAPTER 5. FACEBOOK AND FRIENDSHIP

1. Mingyang Liu. "Duke: Writing on the Wall: Duke Freshmen 'Friend' Early on Facebook Site." *America's Intelligence Wire*, 31 Aug. 2005, ft.com. Accessed 17 July 2018.

2. Liu, "Duke: Writing on the Wall."

3. David Kirkpatrick. *The Facebook Effect*. Simon, 2010. 92.

4. Kirkpatrick, *The Facebook Effect*, 12.

5. Kelly Christ. "Escaping My Addiction to Social Media." *UWire*, 28 Jan. 2018, uwire.com. Accessed 17 July 2018.

6. Graham G. Scott. "More Than Friends: Popularity on Facebook and Its Role in Impression Formation." *Journal of Computer-Mediated Communication*, vol. 19, no. 3, 2014, 365.

7. Scott, "More Than Friends," 361.

8. Katherine Hobson. "Feeling Lonely? Too Much Time on Social Media May Be Why." *National Public Radio*, 6 Mar. 2017, npr.org. Accessed 17 July 2018.

9. Robin Dunbar. "The Limit of Friendship." *The London Times*, 8 Feb. 2010, thetimes.co.uk. Accessed 17 July 2018.

10. Tara Baharamour. "Teens Who Spend Less Time in Front of Screens Are Happier— Up to a Point, New Research Shows." *Washington Post*, 22 Jan. 2018, washingtonpost.com. Accessed 17 July 2018.

11. Jean M. Twenge, Gabrielle N. Martin, and W. Keith Campbell. "Decreases in Psychological Well-Being Among American Adolescents after 2012 and Links to Screen Time During the Rise of Smartphone Technology." *Emotion*, 2018, 13.

12. Alix Langone. "Ex Google and Facebook Employees Are Banding Together to Protect Kids from Social Media Addiction." *Time*, 14 Feb. 2018, time.com. Accessed 17 July 2018.

CHAPTER 6. PRIVACY AND SHARING

1. Graham Meikle and Sherman Young. *Media Convergence*. Palgrave Macmillan, 2012. 73.

2. Meikle and Young, *Media Convergence*, 129.

3. "Kaplan Test Prep Survey: College Admissions Officers Say Social Media Increasingly Affects Applicants' Changes." *Kaplan Test Prep*, 10 Feb. 2017. press.kaptest.com. Accessed 13 Mar. 2018.

4. Alessandra Potenza. "Guess Who's Looking at Your Facebook Page?" *New York Times*, 6 Oct. 2014, nytimes.com. Accessed 17 July 2018.

5. Cara McGoogan. "Facebook Facing Deluge of Complaints over Revenge Porn." *Daily Telegraph*, 23 May 2017, telegraph.co.uk. Accessed 17 July 2018.

6. Kimberly Miller. "Cyberbullying and Its Consequences." *Southern California Interdisciplinary Law Journal*, 26, 2, 2017, 384.

7. Namwan Leavell. "Column: Chronic Relationship Posting Is Exhibitionist." *UWire*, 22 Jan. 2016, uwire.com. Accessed 17 July 2018.

8. Sherisse Pham. "How Facebook Decides What Violent and Explicit Content Is Allowed." *CNN*, 22 May 2017, cnn.com. Accessed 17 July 2018.

CHAPTER 7. A TOOL FOR SOCIAL CHANGE

1. Bobby Ghosh. "Rage, Rap and Revolution." *Time*, 17 Feb. 2011, time.com. Accessed 17 July 2018.

2. Rebecca J. Rosen. "So, Was Facebook Responsible for the Arab Spring after All?" *Atlantic*, 3 Sept. 2011, theatlantic.com. Accessed 19 Mar. 2018.

3. "Arab Spring: 10 Unpredicted Outcomes." *BBC News*, 13 Dec. 2013, bbc.com. Accessed 19 Mar. 2018.

4. Dustin Kidd. *Social Media Freaks*. Westview, 2017. 147–148.

5. Ben Berkowitz. "From a Single Hashtag, a Protest Circled the World." *Reuters*, 17 Oct. 2011, reuters.com. Accessed 19 Mar. 2018.

6. Kidd, *Social Media Freaks*, 158.

7. "Why Do US Police Keep Killing Unarmed Black Men?" *BBC News*, 26 May 2015, bbc.com. Accessed 19 Mar. 2018.

8. Melissa Harris-Perry. "Role Model for Resistance." *Nation*, 15 Sept. 2014, thenation.com. Accessed 17 July 2018.

9. Brian Stelter. "Philando Castile and the Power of Facebook Live." *CNN*, 7 July 2016, cnn.com. Accessed 17 July 2018.

10. Heather Kelly. "Facebook's Zuckerberg Condemns Hate Groups." *CNN*, 16 Aug. 2017, cnn.com. Accessed 17 July 2018.

11. Julia Carrie Wong, Sam Leven, and Olivia Solon. "Bursting the Facebook Bubble." *Guardian*, 16 Nov. 2016, theguardian.com. Accessed 17 July 2018.

12. Heather Kelly. "Hate Groups on Facebook: Why Some Get to Stay." *CNN*, 17 Aug. 2017, cnn.com. Accessed 17 July 2018.

13. Imran Awan. "Cyber-Extremism." *Social Science and Public Policy*, vol. 54, no. 2, 2017, 138.

CHAPTER 8. "BUILDING THE WORLD WE ALL WANT"

1. Mark Zuckerberg. "Building Global Community." *Facebook*, 16 Feb. 2017, facebook.com. Accessed 17 July 2018.

2. Olivia Solon. "It's Digital Colonialism." *Guardian*, 27 July 2017, theguardian.com. Accessed 3 May 2018.

3. Zuckerberg, "Building Global Community."

4. Zuckerberg, "Building Global Community."

5. Matt Stevens and Daniel Victor. "Did Facebook Really Need a Safety Check in New York?" *New York Times*, 1 Nov. 2017, nytimes.com. Accessed 3 May 2018.

6. Hayley Tsukayama. "Here's What Facebook Is Doing with Your Safety Check Data." *Washington Post*, 7 June 2017, washingtonpost.com. Accessed 17 July 2018.

7. Scott Sutherland. "Nowhere to Hide." *NFPA Journal*, Nov./Dec. 2017, nfpa.org. Accessed 26 Mar. 2018.

8. Josh Constine. "Facebook Drops Fee on Donation, Will Match $50M/Year, Adds Mentor Feature." *TechCrunch*, 29 Nov. 2017, techcrunch.com. Accessed 24 Mar. 2018.

9. Constine, "Facebook Drops Fee on Donation."

10. Naomi Gleit. "Facebook Social Good Forum." *Facebook*, 29 Nov. 2017, newsroom. fb.com. Accessed 24 Mar. 2018.

11. Andrew F. Smith. *Rescuing the World*. SUNY, 2010. 42.

CHAPTER 9. FIXING FACEBOOK

1. Scott Shane and Vindu Goel. "Fake Russian Facebook Accounts Bought $100,000 in Political Ads." *New York Times*, 6 Sept. 2017, nytimes.com. Accessed 17 July 2018.

2. Steve Kovach. "Mark Zuckerberg's Personal Challenge for 2018." *Business Insider*, 4 Jan. 2018, businessinsider.com. Accessed 17 July 2018.

3. Lindsey Bever. "Zuckerberg Pledges to Fix Issues with Facebook in 2018." *Washington Post*, 4 Jan. 2018, washingtonpost.com. Accessed 17 July 2018.

4. Sheera Frenkel and Katie Benner. "To Stir Discord in 2016, Russians Turned Most Often to Facebook." *New York Times*, 17 Feb. 2018, nytimes.com. Accessed 20 Mar. 2018.

5. Oprah Winfrey. "Oprah Follows Up with the Partisan Voters in Michigan." *60 Minutes*, 18 Feb. 2018, cbsnews.com. Accessed 20 Mar. 2018.

6. Nicky Woolf. "How Facebook Ate the World." *New Statesman*, 5 Jan. 2018, newstatesman.com. Accessed 17 July 2018.

7. Colin Stretch. "Are Corporations and Government Doing Enough to Counteract Foreign Intervention in Social Media?" *Congressional Digest*, 1 Mar. 2018, congressionaldigest.com. Accessed 17 July 2018.

8. Marty Swant. "Facebook Is Hiring 1,000 People to Review Ads and Monitor Targeting." AdWeek, 2 Oct. 2017, adweek.com. Accessed 6 Aug. 2018.

9. Alvin Chang. "The Facebook and Cambridge Analytica Scandal, Explained with a Simple Diagram." *Vox*, 23 Mar. 2018, vox.com. Accessed 25 Mar. 2018.

10. Aja Romano. "The Facebook Data Breach Wasn't a Hack. It Was a Wake-Up Call." *Vox*, 20 Mar. 2018, vox.com. Accessed 26 Mar. 2018.

11. Olivia Solon. "Facebook Says Cambridge Analytica May Have Gained 37K More Users' Data." *Guardian*, 4 Apr. 2018, theguardian.com. Accessed 4 May 2018.

12. Robert Lemos. "Fake News Campaigns to Increase in Frequency, Security Experts Say." *Eweek*, 4 Dec. 2016, eweek.com. Accessed 17 July 2018.

13. Nick Statt. "Mark Zuckerberg Apologizes for Facebook's Data Privacy Scandal in Full Page Newspaper Ads." *Verge*, 25 Mar. 2018, theverge.com. Accessed 25 Mar. 2018.

14. Nick Statt. "Zuckerberg: 'Move Fast and Break Things' Isn't How Facebook Operates Anymore." *CNET*, 30 Apr. 2014, cnet.com. Accessed 26 Mar. 2018.

15. Sandy Parakilas. "Facebook Wants to Fix Itself. Here's a Better Solution." *Wired*, 30 Jan. 2018, wired.com. Accessed 26 Mar. 2016.

16. Zach Wichter. "2 Days, 10 Hours, 600 Questions." *New York Times*, 12 Apr. 2018, nytimes.com. Accessed 4 May 2018.

17. Kif Leswing. "Nearly One in 10 Americans Surveyed Say They Deleted Their Facebook Account." *Business Insider*, 12 Apr. 2018, businessinsider.com, 4 May 2018.

18. Abrar Al-Heeti. "Mark Zuckerberg Says It Will Take 3 Years to 'Fix' Facebook." *CBS News*, 1 May 2018, cbsnews.com. Accessed 4 May 2018.

19. Alfred Ng. "Facebook's New Dating Service Hopes Love Conquers All, Even Privacy Issues." *CNET*, 3 May 2018, cnet.com. Accessed 4 May 2018.

INDEX

ABOUT THE AUTHOR

GAIL RADLEY

Gail Radley is the author of 29 books for young people and numerous articles for adults. She also teaches English part time at Stetson University in DeLand, Florida, where she lives.